Looking at Rocks

by Elizabeth Moore

Table of Contents

Consultant:
Adria F. Klein, Ph.D.
California State University, San Bernardino

capstone
classroom

Heinemann Raintree • Red Brick Learning
division of Capstone

Rocks Everywhere

Rocks are everywhere.

You can see rocks in the park.

Let's look at rocks up close.

Rocks are in rivers and lakes.

Rock covers our Earth.
Mountains are made of rocks.

Some beaches have small rocks.
Other beaches have sand.
Sand is rock, too.

The Story of Earth

Rocks tell us the story of Earth.
They show where rock was worn
down by water.

The lines of color in the rock show how Earth changed over time.

Rain, wind, and ice made
this rock arch.

Cold and hot weather made
these rock joints.

Some rocks have traces
of animals and plants in them.
These are called fossils.

We can find out when these plants
and animals lived by looking
at fossils.

Using Rocks

People use rocks. They build houses out of rocks. Crushed rocks are used to build roads, tunnels, bridges, airports, and parking lots.

People use rocks to make statues
and decorate buildings.

Rocks for making jewelry
can be found all over the world.
Kings and queens use rocks
in their jewelry.

Rocks are even used at school. Graphite is a rock. It is the part of the pencil that makes a mark.

Rocks are interesting.
Take the time to look at rocks!